ANIMALS

PAUL MASON

Meet Snappy.

Snappy is a young Nile crocodile.

Most crocodiles are only interested in eating and sleeping, but Snappy is different.

Snappy is interested in science, too.

Please visit our website, www.garethstevens.com. For a free color catalog of all our high-quality books, call toll free 1-800-542-2595 or fax 1-877-542-2596.

Cataloging-in-Publication Data
Names: Mason, Paul.
Title: Animals / Paul Mason.
Description: Buffalo, NY : Gareth Stevens Publishing, 2026. | Series: Quick-fix science | Includes glossary and index.
Identifiers: ISBN 9781482473841 (pbk.) | ISBN 9781482473858 (library bound) | ISBN 9781482473865 (ebook)
Subjects: LCSH: Animals--Juvenile literature.
Classification: LCC QL49.M376 2026 | DDC 590--dc23

Published in 2026 by
Gareth Stevens Publishing
2544 Clinton St.
Buffalo, NY 14224

First published in Great Britain in 2021 by Wayland

Design: www.squareandcircus.co.uk

Editor: Nicola Edwards

Cover and interior Snappy artwork by John Haslam

Picture acknowledgements:
Shutterstock: Adike 4c; Africa Studio 28t, 29tcl; Carlos Aguilera 15cl; Alter-ego 29tl; AndreAnita 19cr; Andrew Angelov 15b; Asjoshipphotos 29cr; Natalia Bachkova 3tr, 4bc; B-D-S Piotr Marcinski 5br; Willyam Bradberry 18b; Volodymyr Burdiak 8-9c; Charnsitr 6br, 7bc; Matt Cole 25tl; Connull 17bc; Kiki Dohmeier 10;Natalia Dralova 25c; Tatiana Dyuvbanova 21b; Bruce Eliis 9br; ESB professional 5cl; Joe Farah 20; FiledImage 13cr; Iakov Filimonov 9cl; FilippoPH 19cl; Florida 17bl; Gorillaimages 28br; Andrey Gudkov 11cl; Tero Hakala 17br; Pawel Horzay 28bl; Vitali Hulai 24cr; Olga_i 6-7c; Eric Isselee front cover tl & b, 4cr, 5c, 22t, 31; Andrea Izzotti 13cl; V Jaroslava 3l,9t; Matt Jeppson 21t; Jgorzynik 22b; Kjersti Joergensen 11br; Michal_K 14t; Keattikorn 29cl; FtLaud 15c; Oliver Laurent Photos 4br; LittlePerfectStock 5cr; Liza54500 27br; Viktor Loki 23br; Maria Spb 1, 12-13c; Milart 7bl; Moosehenderson 17t; Neirfly front cover c; Narupon Nimpaiboon 19br; Ninjaudom 6bc; Nuruddean 12bc; Carrie Olson 11t; Onair 28c; Ed Philips 29br; Photoobject front cover tr; Photoongraphy 5bl; Philip Pilosian 19t; Pixelheld 7br; PVLGT 4cl; pixelnest 29bl; Rbrown10 13bl; Tony Rix 11cr; RLS Photo 13t; Jason Patrick Ross 23bc; Stefanek Rostislav 15cr; Jakub Rutkiewicz 14b; Ben Schonewille 23t; B Sekar 15tl; Petr Simon 18t, 30t; J Sineenuch 9cr; Andrew A Skolnick 25tr; Slowmotiongli 19bl; Jeff Starmer 13br; Anna Subbotina 25bl; Tarpan 12bl; Vagabond54 23bl; Olga Vasik 15tr; Frans van Veen 11bl; Anna Maria Vittoria 4bl; Vkilikov 5t;Vasyl Vovk 28bc; Jeffry Weymier 16;Vladimir Wrangel 5bc.

Other contributers:
Ab H Baas/Saxifraga Foundation, CC BY-NC-SA 26-27c.
Judy Gallagher/Wikimedia Commons CCA2.0 27bl.
Peter van der Sluljs/Wikimedia Commons GNUFDL 2.1, CC A SA 4.0 24cl.

Printed in the United States of America

CPSIA compliance information: Batch #CSGS26: For further information contact Gareth Stevens at 1-800-542-2595.

CONTENTS

ANIMAL PLANET

This book is about one of my favorite subjects: animals. It is about all kinds of animals, not just the ones I snack on!

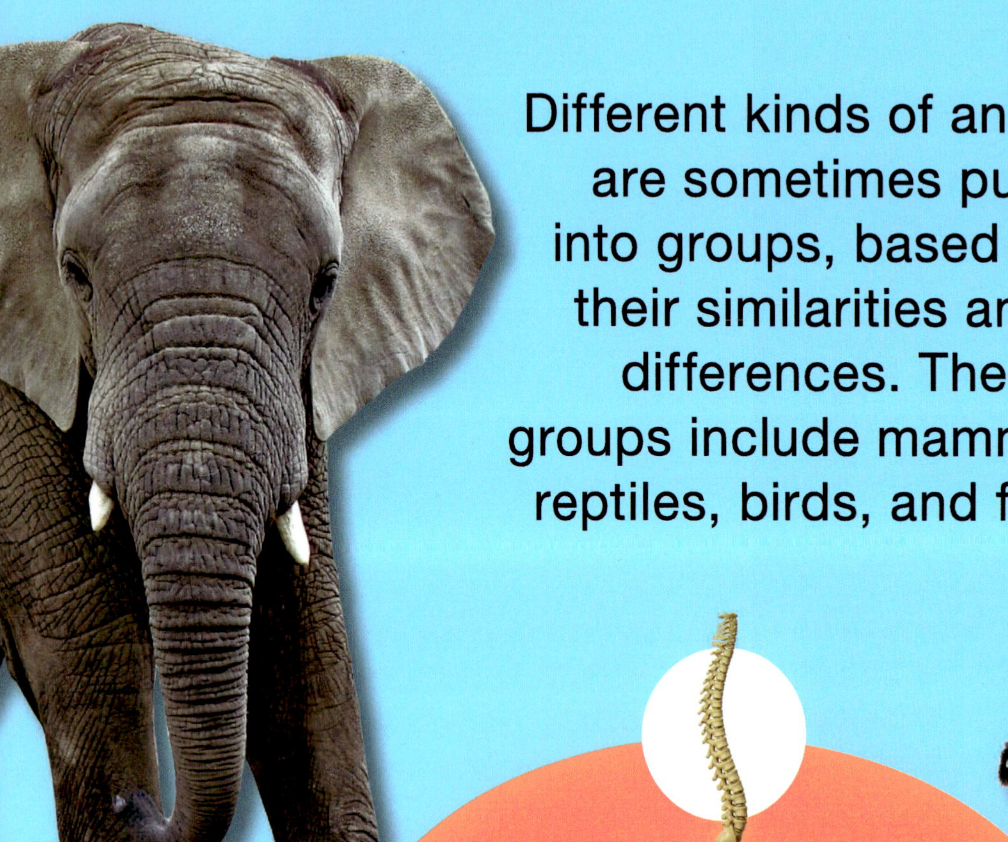

Different kinds of animal are sometimes put into groups, based on their similarities and differences. The groups include mammals, reptiles, birds, and fish.

Backbone

Animal groupings start with whether or not they are vertebrates, which have a backbone. Which of these six animals do?

Snail

Bird

Spider

This book is about different kinds of animals. You will discover what they are like and the special ways they are **adapted** to where they live.

Crocodile

Octopus

Human

The answers are on page 31.

ANIMAL DIET:

WHAT ANIMALS EAT

Personally, there's nothing I like to eat more than meat. Unless it's a bit of fish! Of course, not all animals have the same taste as me.

Menu

Chomp chomp!

All animals need food for energy and to grow. Some animals only eat meat, or only plants. Some animals eat both.

Food goes in and is chewed in the mouth.

Animals have different kinds of poop depending on how their digestion works.

A

B

An animal's body removes **nutrients** from food. These are needed for energy and growth. This process is called **digestion.**

Food is churned up in stomach and becomes liquid.

Nutrients are removed and the liquid becomes solid.

Poop leaves the body.

The last nutrients and water are removed.

What goes in, must come out. Once everything useful has been removed from food, what's left is pushed out as poop.

C

D

E

Did you recognize any of these? Find out whose they are on page 31.

PREDATORS:
SALTWATER CROCODILE

Most meat eaters are predators, like me and my saltwater crocodile relatives from Australia. We **predators** hunt for our food.

Crocodiles are reptiles. Like most reptiles, they have scaly skin and lay eggs. Saltwater crocodiles are the world's biggest reptiles. They are ambush predators. This means they lie in wait for their **prey**.

The biggest saltwater crocodiles weigh more than a small car and are as long as a giraffe is tall.

"Disguise predators" like this scorpion fish blend into the background and pretend they are something else.

"Pursuit predators" like this cheetah chase after their prey.

LAND MAMMALS:
MOUNTAIN GORILLA

A male mountain gorilla can eat over 66 pounds (30 kg) of food a day. That's the same weight as a 10-year-old child. Fortunately, gorillas don't eat 10-year-old children.

A big male gorilla can weigh nearly 441 pounds (200 kg), as much as 2.5 grown men. Female gorillas are much smaller and only weigh half as much. What do they eat to get so big? Roots, stems, leaves, fruit, and even flowers.

Only about 1 percent of a mountain gorilla's food is meat. They get this by eating insects.

Gorillas are mammals. Mammals have hair and breathe air. Their young get milk from their mothers.

Yes please!

I can't think of anything worse than eating vegetables, but it is surprisingly popular.

Which of these do you think eats mostly plants, meat, or both?

Answers on page 31

MARINE MAMMALS:

BLUE WHALE

The blue whale is the world's biggest animal, but that doesn't mean it hunts big prey. In fact, its food is as tiny as the whale is huge.

Whales come to the surface to breathe, but can stay underwater for over 15 minutes.

Blue whales are marine mammals, or mammals which live in water.

The biggest whales can eat up to 4.4 tons (4 mt) of krill a day.

A blue whale eats little shrimplike animals called krill. The krill are only as long as your little finger.

The krill are sometimes deep underwater. The whales can dive down over 328 feet (100 m) to find them.

SEA AND FRESHWATER HABITATS: SALMON

Personally I like to swim in a river, but we're all different. Saltwater crocodiles, for example, like rivers AND the sea. And they're not alone.

Most fish live in salt water or **fresh water**. Some fish, though, can survive in both. Salmon are one of these.

Most fish have fins and scales. They breathe underwater using **gills**.

The salmon have to get past anglers, bears, and other predators.

To have young, salmon travel from the ocean to the rivers where they hatched.

They also have to leap up waterfalls and past dams.

When they arrive, the salmon are tired out. Most breed, then die.

Atlantic stingray

Eel

Bull shark

Here are some other fish that can survive in both salt water and fresh water.

Green sawfish

BIRDS OF PREY:

BALD EAGLE

My parents told me: "Eat up, if you want to grow big and strong!" (Crocodiles are surprisingly good parents compared to other reptiles.) Maybe that's how this next animal got to be so mighty.

Eagles are birds. Birds have beaks, feathers, wings, legs, and they lay eggs.

Their excellent eyesight helps the bald eagle spot fish.

After swooping down, their talons grab a slippery fish.

Bald eagles love to eat salmon. Some people call salmon a "superfood," because it is so full of nutrients. The eagles are especially good at hunting salmon and other fish.

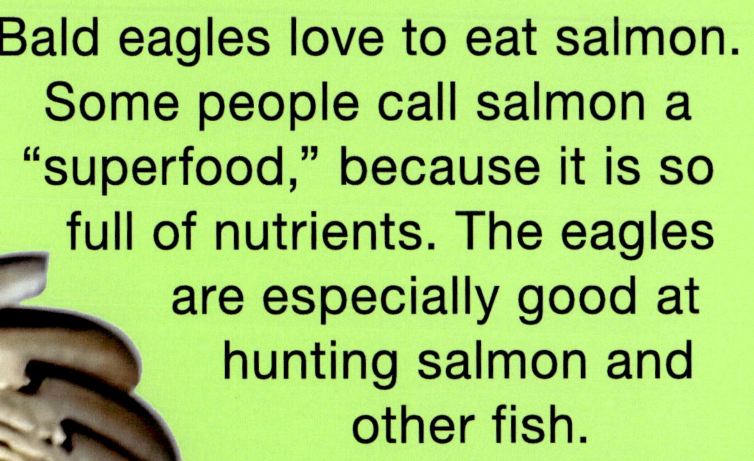

Their sharp, curved beaks tears off strips of flesh.

How are these birds adapted for hunting? There are some clues here, and answers on page 31.

Merlins hunt small, fast-moving birds.

Owls hunt at night.

Ospreys dive in to catch fish.

MIGRATION:
ARCTIC TERN

My short legs aren't really made for long-distance travel, so I find this next animal's long journeys awe-inspiring.

Arctic terns are small birds, but they make the longest journeys in the animal world. They fly from the Arctic to the Antarctic and back every year: That's about 55,923 miles (90,000 km).

Arctic terns are not the only animals that make long journeys to find food and water each year:

Great white sharks travel 13,670 miles (22,000 km).

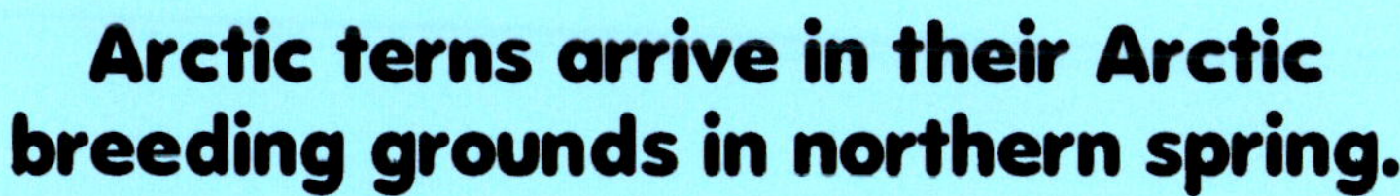
Arctic terns arrive in their Arctic breeding grounds in northern spring.

Nesting regions

Migration routes

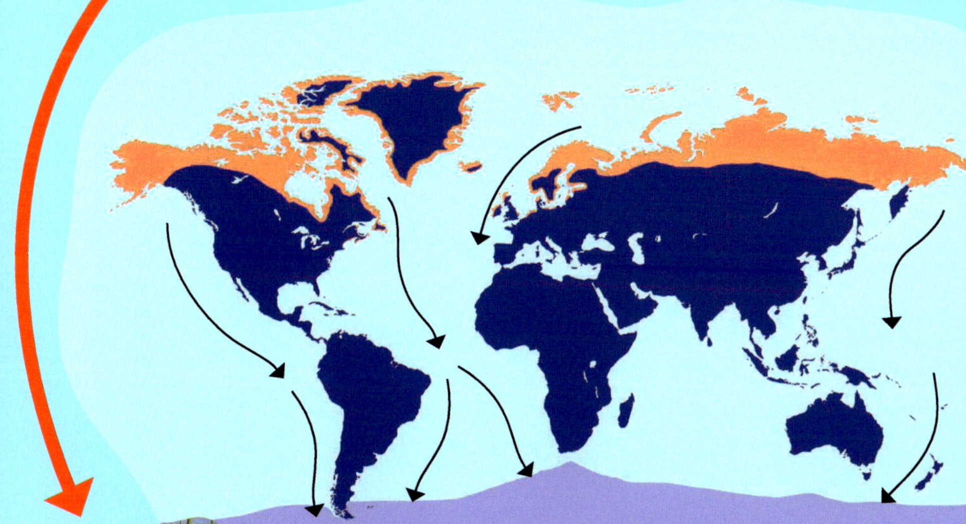

They arrive in time for the Antarctic summer.

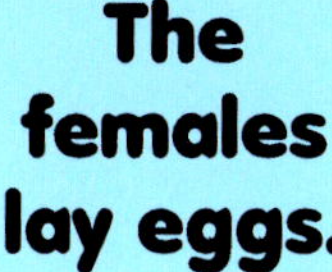
The females lay eggs.

Chicks are fed sand lances by their parents.

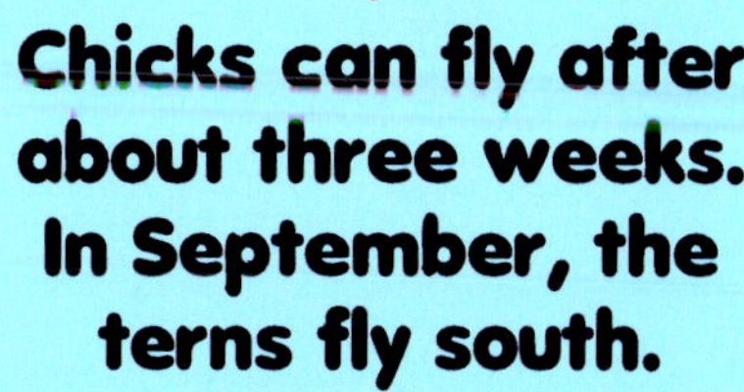
Chicks can fly after about three weeks. In September, the terns fly south.

Blue wildebeest travel 1,864 miles (3,000 km).

Globe skimmer dragonflies journey 11,184 miles (18,000 km) from India to East Africa and back.

AMPHIBIANS:

TIGER SALAMANDER

If I had skin like a tiger salamander's, I'd show it off all the time! Weirdly, though, this animal prefers to spend most of its time underground.

Tiger salamanders are amphibians. Amphibians usually:

1. release their eggs in water
2. breathe underwater using gills when young
3. breathe air using lungs when older.

Tiger salamanders live near ponds and slow-flowing streams.

Tiger salamanders live in underground burrows, where it is never too hot or cold. They come out at night to feast on worms, snails, slugs, and insects.

Amphibians really are a funny bunch! Here's another oddball:

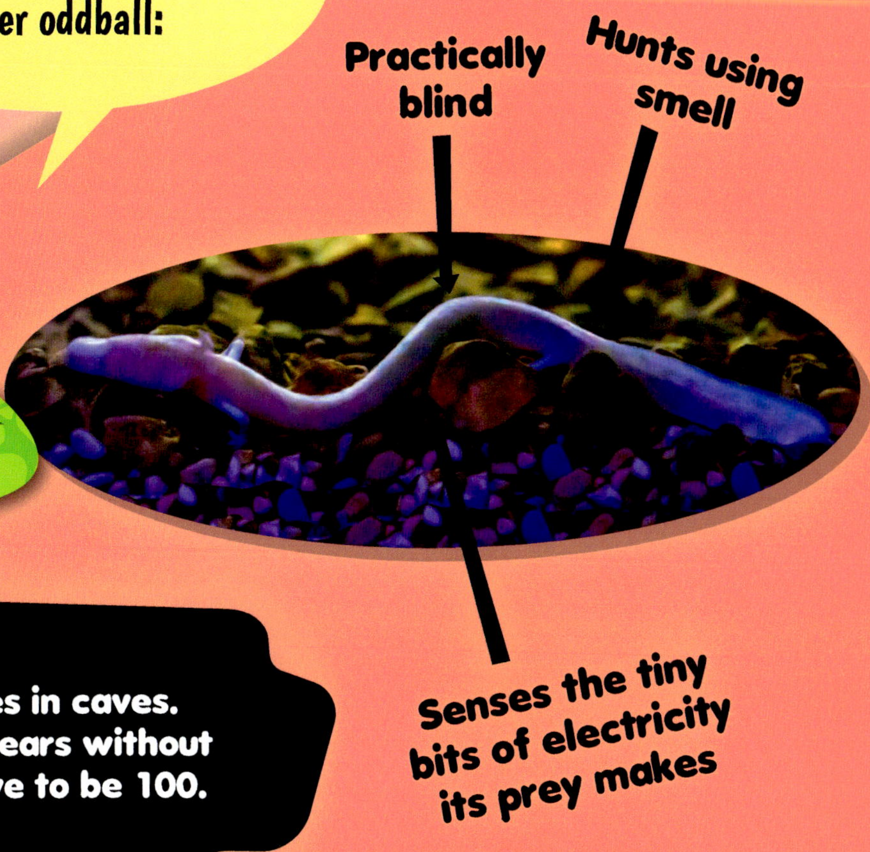

Practically blind

Hunts using smell

Senses the tiny bits of electricity its prey makes

The olm lives in caves. It can go 10 years without eating and live to be 100.

HIBERNATION:

HEDGEHOG

Reptiles like me REALLY don't enjoy the cold. In fact, most animals avoid cold if they can. They either live somewhere that never gets cold, or find a way to hide from it.

European hedgehogs hide from the cold by **hibernating**. They slow down their bodily processes to save energy. When winter comes, they find a sheltered place called a hibernaculum, and curl up.

Lots of other animals hibernate. One of these does it in large groups. Can you guess which?

Box turtle

Once a hedgehog is curled up:

1. its body temperature drops

2. its heart slows down

3. it lives off fat stored up through summer.

Common poorwill

Garter snake

Wood frog

Answers on page 31.

LIFE CYCLES:

DRAGONFLY

Crocodiles can live for about as long as humans, so I feel a bit sorry for dragonflies, whose whole life lasts less than a year.

Dragonflies are insects. Insects have three pairs of legs, and bodies divided into head, thorax, and abdomen. They have an **exoskeleton** instead of a backbone.

One week later, eggs hatch into nymphs.

Nymphs live underwater.

Female lays eggs in water.

	In existence for	Lifespan
DRAGONFLIES	300,000,000 years	6 months
CROCODILES	200,000,000 years	70-100 years
HUMANS	200,000 years	70-100 years

Months later, the nymph climbs out of the water.
Its exoskeleton splits and a dragonfly appears.
Each time the nymph grows, it sheds its exoskeleton.
The dragonfly's wings dry out. It can take hours, or even days, before the dragonfly flies off.
At first, dragonflies are a pale color. Over time, they begin to look much more colorful.

SPIDERS:

ZEBRA JUMPING SPIDER

We crocodiles often lie in wait, hidden in the water, then leap out to grab our victims. The zebra spider hunts in the same way, just without the water.

The spider creeps close to its prey, disguised by its stripes. When it is within 4 inches (10 cm), it jumps on its prey. This jump is 14 times its body length.

Spiders have four pairs of legs and bodies in two parts. They are **invertebrates**, with an exoskeleton instead of a backbone.

The bolas spider uses a sticky ball on a string of silk.

The raft spider hunts insects and fish at the surface of ponds.

INSECTS:

BEES

Most people know that bees make honey. But can you guess which of these other foods bees help make? The answer is on page 31.

Pollination and Plants

Pollination is how plants grow and spread. It happens when tiny grains called pollen are swapped from one plant to another, usually by insects.

I'm buzzing!

The plant releases chemicals to attract bees.

A bee lands on flower, begins to drink nectar, and pollen sticks to the bee.

At the next flower, pollen is brushed off of the bee.

The number of bees on Earth is falling. Chemicals on our crops kill insects such as bees. There are also fewer places for bees to live.

We can help bees by growing plants that they like:

Summer: bees love lavender.

Autumn:
abelia is sometimes called the "bee bush"

Spring:
apple blossoms

Early winter:
ivy, a last meal before bees hibernate

GLOSSARY

adapt change in a way that works better than before

blossom flower or group of flowers, usually found on a tree or bush

digestion removing the things that a body needs from the food it eats

exoskeleton hard outer shell that gives some animals shape and protection. Crabs, shellfish, insects, and spiders all have exoskeltons

fresh water water that is not salty. Fresh water is found in rivers and lakes.

gill body part that can remove oxygen from water (like our lungs removing oxygen from air). Gills allow some animals to breathe underwater.

hibernate go into a sleeplike state during cold weather

invertebrates animals without a backbone

nectar sugary liquid found in many plants. The plants use nectar to attract insects such as bees.

nutrient something the body needs to be able to stay alive and grow

predator animal that hunts other animals for food

prey animal that is hunted by other animals

vertebrates animals with a backbone

ANSWERS

Page 4 The bird, crocodile, and human have backbones. They are vertebrates. The snail, spider and octopus do not. They are invertebrates.

Page 7
a) cow pat, b) dog poop, c) rabbit poop, d) bird poop and e) wombat poop. No one really knows for sure why wombat poops are square-shaped.

Page 11
Camel, plants; iguana, plants (mostly leaves); sandpiper, meat (insects, worms, and mollusks); porcupine, plants; otter, meat.

Page 17
The owl needs to hear prey in the dark. The shape of an owl's face helps it do this.

A merlin needs to make fast changes of direction. Its narrow wings are good for this.

The osprey sometimes needs to put its face underwater. It has an extra eyelid to protect its eyes, and can even close its nostrils to stop water from getting in.

Page 23
Garter snakes hibernate in large groups of hundreds, or even thousands, of snakes. They do this to keep each other warm. Garter snakes are mostly harmless, but you still would not want to put your foot in a group of hibernating ones.

Page 28
All of them! Bees help pollinate most of the fruit and vegetables we eat. Some crops, such as almonds, are ONLY pollinated by bees.

FINDING OUT MORE

Books to read

Forrester, Philippa. *Amazing Animal Journeys.* London, England: Dorling Kindersley, 2023.

MacCarald, Clara. *Getting Smelly to Survive.* Minneapolis, MN: Kid Core, 2023.

McHale, Benda. *Animals in the Air.* New York, NY: Enslow Publishing, 2023.

Websites to visit

zooborns.com
If you like baby animals, you will love this website, which has photos of newly born animals from zoos and aquariums around the world. Want to know what a baby otter, octopus, or owl looks like? This is the place to find out.

kids.nationalgeographic.com/animals/
There is absolutely loads of information here, organized between mammals, birds, reptiles, amphibians, invertebrates (animals without backbones), and fish. Some of the words are quite difficult, but there are excellent videos of some of the animals.

worldwildlife.org/species
This is great place to find out about some of the threats animals are under. You can look up specific animals, find out about endangered species, and even play animal trivia games.

INDEX